More Praise for *Wake-Up Calls*

"Wanda Phipps's words are illuminated and clear, grounded, able to disappear and reappear, map the body and the city's common spaces. These meditations ground us and explode us. *Wake-Up Calls: 66 Morning Poems* is a terrific book."
—**Joseph Lease**

"Wanda Phipps's new book gracefully navigates an expedition through interrupted dreams, soft-focus adventures and the rush hour that often occurs between four walls. Slightly hazy, sometimes hormonal, these poems entice the reader into imagining what's really going on—between the lines. A truly beautiful and inspiring work."
—**Gillian McCain**

Wake-Up Calls

Wake-Up Calls:
66 Morning Poems

Wanda Phipps

Soft Skull Press
2004

Published by Soft Skull Press
71 Bond Street, Brooklyn, NY 11217

Distributed by Publishers Group West
800.788.3123 | www.pgw.com

Cataloging-in-Publication Data for this
title available from the Libray of Congress

I'd like to thank the editors of *BoogLit*,
Boston Poetry Marathon 2003 Postcard Set,
the *Broadshirt Poetry Magazine*,
TheEastVillage.com, How2, Isibongo,
Milkmag, papertiger, the *Portable Boog
Reader, Salon.com*, and *Zither Mood*, where
some of these poems previously appeared.

Printed in Canada

Thanks to Joel Schlemowitz, Carol Schlemowitz, Josette Urso, Pamela Joy, Alison Davis, John S. Hall, Lewis Warsh, Andrei Codrescu, David Kirschenbaum, Daniela Gioseffi, Joseph Lease, Hilton Obenzinger, Joan Steinau Lester, Shanna Compton, Richard Nash, David Janik, Daniel Nester, and all of the Soft Skull team.

MORNING POEM #1

floating gray web pages
step into a crowded vacuum
clouds sweating

there's a gauzy scrim
in front of my eyes
between me and
the rest of the world

afternoon birds

MORNING POEM #2
AGAIN & AGAIN

morning sounds
birds
coughing
secret creaks in floors
ceiling
hidden parts
garbage trucks
wake-up groans
hearts suspended
mid-dream

planes hover
daytime sneaks in
with a slowly
building clarity
a slight pain also
still stubborn
persistent time
moves
continually placing
one moment after the next
keeping all from seeing
all things
from happening
at once

stepping in again
stories we play over
and over
top ten psychic hits
spinning nonstop

my costume tonight
is Max Ernst's
half bird, half woman

half in a waking state
half asleep
part in the moment before this
and part in the moment to come
flight takes me
or rather wakes me up
to where I can speak

MORNING POEM #3

vodka still moves through me
wind bangs the venetians against the sill
and thoughts of you

reimagine your back through the bathroom
door high white light rounding your
   shoulders
now candlelight carves sweet shadows

in your face. voice/sounds like rough
   handling
deep strokes and sure focus
bring me back to me

and you and a separate space
ours in the ease of lingering pauses
or the rush of our seconds passing

MORNING POEM #4

howdy, ranger
howdy, my warm
down jacket voice
my dreams were full
of intrigue last night
politics: I was kidnapped
by some radical types
but my love of freedom
was stronger than
their rhetoric and
though you could
have rescued me
I escaped on my own
somehow by my wits
but soon found myself
missing my captor/companions
my comrades in anarchy

my golden angel wakes before me
this is his big day
to exhibit his fine objects
art on parade
but first he goes to
help another artworker
bring his visions alive
I stay snuggled in bed
a perfect fool
last night he
gave me a gift
of black raspberry jam
from his apple picking
trip to Hastings on the Hudson
with the Aesthesians
when I preferred to remain
cloistered, chained to
my desk and spent all
day and most of the night
trying to work
and dodging tiny
pinpricks of jealousy
and suspicion
last night he cooked me
dinner again and I
examined the words and
music of Suzanne Vega's
new watered-down pop/

desiccated folk while he
shot the last five feet of
a roll for a film screening
this weekend
after late night TV
and our little talk
of group marriage
and giggles—the dark
found his hands
between my legs
as he told me a story
where he was the costar
with me and another man
and they both graced me
with ecstasy—I listened
with my hands between
my legs—my angel's fingers
inside me—his satin voice
in my ear and hand
like heavy ether
on my breasts
Chelsea traffic, horns, car alarms
wake me this morning
as my angel kisses me goodbye
already I miss him and another
as I snuggle warm in bed
I am a perfect fool

MORNING POEM #6

groggy voice
hangover head
phone rings
work call
money writing
muddled thoughts
adrenaline rush
hands clutch
power book
pauses come
rapid doubts
make calls
take notes
mind push
fear waits

MORNING POEM #7

last night I went
to a place I haven't
visited in dreams
in years
it's San Francisco
second-floor apartment
with bay windows
onto a busy
commercial street
I've never lived there
but in sleep it is my home
a lot of pain happened
there but I can't
remember the details
so catching only a glimpse
of it last night
frightened me

body heavy
from the waist down
but overall
contentment

the single mother
screams at her kids
across the way

dogs bark in morning
visitors as my
honey sleeps

and my mind
juggles lists
of things to do

things needing
to be done needing
mind space

MORNING POEM #9
YOM KIPPUR

7 a.m. alarm
morning chill
and head clouds
rush to make
the rush-hour rush
to work for the
National Football League
change my mind about
the floral print dress
chosen last night
slacks too wrinkled
so I go with the long
black skirt, big black
blouse, black sweater
against the morning
chill under tan man's
blazer and my favorite
black lace-up boots
under me
hair's wild today
but don't feel like
reining it in
although I manage
to make a semi-
made-up face
as armor against
hostile commuters

and the corporate crowd
miss St. Croix and
the sudden downpours
with the sun still out
as I go through
another office day
I slowly begin to
hide myself
behind a mask
of pleasant indifference

MORNING POEM #10

I am part of a history
fitful sleep last night
woke from my own
moans and deadline
anxiety early
now I try to write
concise—edit down
the world
and those ever-present
birds sing to me
I am part of a history
of North Carolina farm workers
grand storytelling office workers
creative patient teachers
Texas backwoods cow herders
ranting alcoholic preachers
and spit shined military men
I am part of a history
of Cherokee mixed marriages
and European and African lovers
I am part of a history
of raging political poets
of boho babies in exile
of round pegs carvin'
those round (w)holes
I am part of a history
still burning through
me on a hazy Loisaida morning

still making me
history still in the making
in me
and those goddamn crazy birds

full of too much sensation
thoughts also
lifting heavy objects
to benefit the arts
cramming facts
in paragraphs
for art and profit
dizzy on a cool
September morning
dizzy with the sound
of angel coming
hands on my breasts
thoughts like heavy
objects juggling
through too much
of everything

MORNING POEM #12

there's a slight drizzle
as we walk down
the gray bike path
under bending branches
by the creek

an unlikely tribe
we travel in a pack
making elusive
alliances

on our way to poetry
summer camp
we stop to take
a photo
document the
moment

as a rainbow
hovers over us
our bold banner
an omen
a blessing

MORNING POEM #13

Saturn eclipsed
the moon last night
heavy thoughts tears
hormone crash again
editor's wake-up call
wanting more info
in ten minutes
try to get it end
up getting friend angry
cursing

call another
for possible solace in song
fiddler folk singer
grand heart
talk of coffee versus tea
and his dream
of finding in the woods
a lost town—all alive
as they were 300
years ago
a huge barn that goes
on forever
and a siphon from the creek
funneled to a trough
where a gigantic slug
lives
maybe the water he thinks

something in the water
has kept the town alive
for all these years
I ask if he has Leadbelly tapes
afraid to ask to jam with him
hang up the phone and cry
water on my cheeks
maybe something in it

MORNING POEM #14

finally conscious enough
brain working enough
just rising at 4:21 p.m.
Saturday park
full of characters
stimulation overload
rain's coming
park-dwellerspeak:
"like my father
always told me
treat every man
like a king
every woman
like a queen
every child
an heir apparent"

MORNING POEM #15

blank subway faces
mouths and eyes at rest
fire could ignite them
on a ride through the
unconscious tunnel
one thing not
following another

MORNING POEM #16

eyes' language
as crazed god
not the art
but the nouveau
happy park
awful foreign
reason tired
tour unlearned

phone rings
wake up
"were you sleeping"
"no"
lie
"yes"
truth
"I see Sigourney Weaver
on the cover not you
—I'll look again"
"yeah, look again"

so far so mortgaged
soon you'll know
dubious powers
they say squarely
you keep Dali fashion
high inclinations
points look resourceful
gains protect your
birth wings don't
cycle solitaire pick
damn destiny
remember carefully
fresh lunar harvest

other notes:
filming of *The Real Blonde*
on gritty streets of Lower East Side
(East Seventh Street between First & A)
artists telling freelance horror
stories of Denmark
and several jury-duty
nightmare remembrances
curl into my cool October
NYNEX billing office line
and irritable Pakistani
hardware store clerks
copy the clips, fix the lamp
pick up the mail, answer the phone
write those letters, gather the gossip
and in-between the
real life and televised
soaps read Ginsberg and Anne Rice

another dream of rooms
foreign rooms
secret rooms
peopled by strangers
blindly moving

freezing loft
I wear a peacock
feather in my hair
to match his
new Purple
Haze Manic
Panic streak
through blonde
strands
anxiety gives
in to a slowing
downswing
try to intercede
with phone calls
and zillion messages
to callous answering
machine voices
in search of verbal
contact—a conversation
of real import
or light engaging
gossip—last night
a dread of socializing
some intuitional
omen of something
bad happening if
I went someplace
I was expected

fooled fate with
a run in the other
direction—now seeking
one-on-one confessions
procrastination pushing
away those pesky
business letters
waiting to be written
those complex but
emotionally lacking
articles—those decisions
on submissions of work
of possible rejection
reading newsletters instead
turning the TV off and on
and off again—dreading
the long walk home
with heavy baggage
of work I haven't done

nothing I want
more than nothing
nothing
to fear
to expect
to criticize
to dread
to bore
to struggle against
nothing
no anxiety
no pressure
no disappointment
no unrealistic hopes
no disillusion
no broken hearts
no nostalgic looks
no longing glances
no apocalypse

MORNING POEM #22

sometimes I don't know
where I am
this can't be real
your hands on my thighs
no that seems
like years ago
your voice in my ear
no now I'm alone
with the company
of books, four walls
and windows on bits
of sky thinking what
happened yesterday
and what's planned
for tomorrow but
where am I now
which is real
yesterday, today,
tomorrow or
none of it

afraid of socializing
of awkward glances
of talking too much or too little
of claustrophobia
of failure
of too much pain
of too much joy
leading later
to too much pain
of boredom
of deadlines
of sitting in a restaurant
and seeing a beggar come in
and watching the busboy
push him out the door
with such anger—a Lennon song
playing through the sound system
and a man seeking
shelter from the rain
under awning
jabbed until he gets up
and is told to leave—
I'm afraid that I'm
in collusion with the
bullying busboy because
I'm a patron in this
restaurant—
I'm afraid one day

I'll be that beggar
I cry because I feel
I could be the busboy too
or the owner of the restaurant
and the old man under the
awning—I am all of them

saw a headless pigeon
almost got bitten by
an angry dog tied up
in front of a laundromat
and ran into "squirrel"
once again digging
a hole to hide his nuts
called the police on
a raging teenage boy
about to beat up his girlfriend
he threatened to beat me up too
three police cars circled the block
twice while he hid out in a bar
then ran—no cop got out of his car
or went into the bar until he had
gone—the girlfriend ran in
the other direction

poor people have
no place to be
poor people have
no protection
under US law
poor people
can't afford rights
poor people
can't afford dignity
poor people
can't afford doctors
poor people are disposable
because poor people's value
can't be measured
in dollars

MORNING POEM #26

today is not a day for poetry.

I should have stayed
here with the beautiful
strong cold Corinna Mae
I should have stayed here
all those years ago
with the known and familiar
I shouldn't have called so much
I shouldn't have been so callous
I should have stuck by you
after recovery
I should have moved to DC
when you asked me to
I should have taken that editing job
I should have taken that TV PA job
I should have gone through with
that graduate school acceptance
I should have loved you
when we first met
I should have been a performance poet
a spoken word artist
I should have gone every place
I was afraid to go
I should have helped you find an apartment
I should have been more interesting
and less the clinging vine
I should have protested loudly
about some things and not at
all about others

I should have learned Spanish and German
I shouldn't have been so easily discouraged
I should have listened to my mother
my life could have been so much better
by now

I forgot the time
with old poems
old boxes
old papers
photographs
and the Big Bridge
got the boxes
I hope so
how'd you like
the party
blinds fell down
behind glasses and
stone face—the Brit
not speaking
only watching
evaluation
not enough room
squeezing emptiness
into space
giggles and spankings
old words
old thoughts
the books are packed
and labeled fic/lit
psyche/phil
Homer to use
spirit books
there's a list

and this is another
slightly Japanese
wardrobe and
perfumed soaps
the 3-D glasses in
the photo and the
master of the house
of funk a turntable
unamplified
faux fur turns round
and round where
will the tryst be
this time—who are
the partners
old wine
old looks
a smile can be
not a smile
a kiss not a kiss
but a city
operational I am
with tea and mobility
fall into the rhythm
that's a sure step
old lines
old minds
step on the leather
there's volcanic O.
and she's in the desert
or Rosalind's feather

or Orlando's in the wall
a landscape will
succeed me—outlive me
be me
old ties
old blues
old tune
your machine's in the corner
broke your head on the Moviola
now make the dinner table
new for a new beginning
put another coat of paint on the shelf
old tears
old ways
old baggage
here comes a twister
Annie's prison reports
charred records
cool breeze
cops on the corner
and bullhorns in the park
old name
old news
old fight

Ann-Margaret flies by
from *Bye Bye Birdie*
and I want my
amazing life-sized
inflatable Joel doll
when he's not home
and who are you
red desert and a green valley
you could be there too
what about ranger
in verse and the reversal
of travel after any journey
there is the pause of remembrance
and who would you be without it
and by the by there's a fly on the glass
and a mirror in your eyes

dodged people talking
into the air through their
cellular friends
forgot my Wanda Bra
great advice:
why sort it all out
just throw it all
in a box and move

MORNING POEM #31

pluck the hairs on my tummy
arrange the books by category
call and say the work will be done
call and ask when the check is coming
arrange to turnoff and turnon
what's necessary
file our love letters away
stay focused stick to the point
whatever that could be

MORNING POEM #32

lights out—bruise
on my thigh—balancing
heavy weights—a
weighty move from sector
to sector—from Orion
to superstores—from
Habib's to the Big Cup
from solitary to dual plan
tomorrow: aching back
& more objects to make orderly

MORNING POEM #33
For Joel

he sits one sock on &
one sock off
legs together tight
black cat on his lap
light gray through
window spreads
through dark loft cavern
he's an art saint at home
head haloed by
reels of film

who will take the table piece
not a decoration but a declaration piece
a rocky confession to no one in particular
there was a long narrow hallway
rough stone walls—large stones jutting out
hands grabbing them in the dark
for balance moving slowly through
this tunnel—the stuttering phrases not
meant to be you but only sound
the music of emotional distortion
vocal fuzz box wah wah for the
    meaning/mind
travel takes the forefront foreign places
and a house of many rooms
lost in them—searching
set the table, take my hand
eat at the table, first fuck of the new year
we were all waiting for you at the Gas
    Station
and you were late again after drinking more
than enough wine entering with entourage
    in tow
I'm claustrophobic in these incestuous
    connections
valuing solitude, private spaces

elephantine revving of
Vesuvian engines
towards this gray day
7 a.m. eyes open clear
headed after yesterday's
constant aches and cloudy
brain—reading about Robert
Creeley, vampires, Japanese
noise rock and British trip-hop
small room Sunday morning
quiet is heavy but nice
throw the office clothes
into the suitcase
with the hangers still on
wrap the pots and pans
in plastic bags
place in sturdy plastic
milk crates—the reference
books fall, answering machine,
paperclips, file folders, telephone
and laptop all slide to the floor
after shifting boxes taping
boxes, more clothes in bag
check out *Web Del Sol* on the net
look for PoProj updates: none
did I lose my broken nail file
cinnamon bagel with cream cheese
and raspberry jelly, pears and

Lapsang Souchong tea
Joel calls it wet bark tea
remember dreamscape:
train stations, bus stations
airports—sixth grade move from
Franklin St. to E St. & Benning Rd.
stayed around ten years
here three—now gone again
the place seems smaller with less
here—lonesome bare walls
and empty shelves

working where I
don't know what
they do—answer
the phone "Healthcare"
missed breakfast
snacking on
roasted peanuts
& Coca Cola
remembering the
angry sky
above Houston
& First Avenue
this morning &
a friendly poet
on disability
waving hello over his
Sidewalk Café breakfast

MORNING POEM #37

try on all the shoes
and see if they fit
everyone always leaving
always mourning
the loss of
the loss of
the loss of

joined Bernadette & Phil
on a leisurely stroll
through Loisaida
to check out the
new French eatery
on Avenue B
exchanging gossip
& giggles
as the last fine day
of fall dissolved
into rain although
the man I
gave change to
in front of S.O.K.'s
greeted me with
"Hello, Sunshine"
as always

MORNING POEM #39

if she took off her top
would that embarrass you
would you smile
and laugh nervously
would there be
room on the roof
for the orgy
if the music
was a little louder
would you remember
the color of her eyes

pink around a
circle of pink
around a shimmer
of found reason
pink around a
glimmering white
snaked around
a sound blue
somehow in the
touch of green
looped inside
loops abound
a bound ribbon
a hope bow bows
in a rare season

MORNING POEM #41

today I learned
about Styrofoam
coffins for flowers
surrounded by an
eternal Christmas
in an Indian restaurant
drinking gallons of water
to replace all the sweat
lost lifting boxes
and boxes up and down stairs
now waiting for our
biryani and vindaloo
today I learned about anxiety,
exhaustion, memory, nostalgia
and new births

8:30 a.m. and
I'm a Chelsea girl
overlooking the
Irish Rep
and a lone tree
full of golden leaves
bends in front of
the Greyhound Elevator Corp.
or is it the Metropolitan Elevator Corp.
or is it both
next to the Stanwick Building
leather jacket weather
but already the sun
coming down on
bundled cyclist
hard to imagine after
last night's chilly
post-curry walk
under a ringed
full moon
The Importance of
Being Earnest
posters me
implying intrigue
and mischief all
cattycorner to the Buddhist
Meditation Center
but I have to go sit

at the Big Cup:
second-biggest gay pick-up
joint next to the Barracuda
of course—I'm waiting
for the true mirror

I close my eyes
and there it is
a concrete walkway
leading out of a
small village
hugging the sides
of a green green
tree-filled mountainside
and to the right
a pipe railing
painted the color
of oxidized metal
and even further
to my right
a small beach
coastline—an ocean
all under a pale blue sky
all there when my eyelids
close and the shutters open

MORNING POEM #44

black cat Tristana
sits on angel's computer
wagging tail back
and forth across
the screen—a fuzzy
windshield wiper
keeping time
to Haydn
on the radio

a David died
but which one
they called
to tell me
they mentioned
the title of his book
I didn't want to go
to the memorial
I didn't want to cry

which David was it
the one who'd
just got back
from Japan
the one who
owned the rare
bookstore
or the editor
not the poet?

there was
a tour guide
with a huge glowing
multicolored wand
pointing out
architectural details
to a huge crowd
bussed in from
the burbs perhaps

ran into the violinist
on her bike
on her way home
from her power-
pop rehearsal
we talked about
her Austrian lover
just outside the cybercafe
where I'd just missed
the klezmer concert
after catching the tail end
of the book party
for a filmmaker
who also writes poetry
but in his native tongue
and I don't remember
which language that is
but the book was translated
by another poet
who's also an accountant

and also at the party
was a fiction writer
I hadn't seen in years
a petite pert redhead
married to a Japanese artist
I remember his
big white voluminous
participatory public
sculptures and her story

about cigarettes
or rather the people
who smoke them

wandered around
my newly old neighborhood
having it seem
foreign to me now
as I made my way
Northwest to my
new Chelsea digs
nearly deserted
very dark wide
avenues late at night
ran into angel
on the corner

and now
I'm in the middle
feeling at home
neither here
nor there
knowing someone
everywhere
but never feeling
quite at ease
or ever knowing
which David it was
that died

MORNING POEM #46
HALLOWEEN

"moreover, so much of music as is adapted
to the sound of the voice . . ." Plato, *Timaeus*

woman in white
glides across the floor
above the floor
and more of the automatic
movie as my eyes close
shutters open
woman of the village
by the sea
tree-lined mountainside
and cliffs also
moreover so much
sound as music is

MORNING POEM #47

forgot the poem
and the words
crying again
in a dark cavern evening
sleeping man beside me
head filling with terrors
too many to mention

cold bed
gray day
memories
of "birds of prey"
talk for the sake
of words shaping
mouth moving
thoughts changing
energy moving
outside of self
talk for the sake
of a warm bed
a sunny day
and memories
of birds at play

rocky Sunday
freezing air
yellow walls
screaming
under forest
green fleurs-de-lis
a television disassembled
on the Persian rug
hulking metal, wires & circuitry
measure the supports
reassemble the base
all for glimpses
of dark images
and flickering
bright lights

what's the future?
heaven for
the queen of bingo
or a cozy bed
& breakfast in Lhasa
I've had my daily dose
of warm phone voices
& cool e-mail syllables
& the cheat goes on
a train through the Andes
could be a moonscape to you
but paradise to me
travel as lifestyle
from here to there
as the navigation
between dreams & lies
move from the bed to the door
foot from blanket to floor
one is too many
a step, no a lie
caught on tape
tomorrow voting
for the lesser evil
back to my old drag
to pull the lever
push the future
baby carriage
in my head

transition from
a life once, twice
gone & then again
it happens

waning desire
on election day
"do you think that?
is that what you think?"
two voices on
the machine now
tuning into the
return of the
nineteenth century
"I'll be the one
with the yellow rose"
all things are impossible
your hand on my hand
in the hands of
some wild ecstasy
"I'll speak to you soon"
"let me buy the honey"
belly dancing to the
Velvet Underground
in my *I-Dream-of-Jeannie-*
hairdo—your head in the circuits
his head in the software
my head in between the two
nestle me in with your
voice hoarse in my brain
"let's fuck" dreaming
all the time of China

MORNING POEM #52

most famous poet
in the world
called me today
about sharing
a cab ride
to Brooklyn

birthday full
of wine and tears
red poppies
couscous and broccoli
happy you know what
thirty-six and still here
fears and all
peel off my
long undies
forgot the romantic
candles and the poem too

MORNING POEM #54

pushing crumbling plaster
rearranging sheet metal
in order to
push the tables
fold the burlap
scrub the bathroom floor
another publication
another invitation
will there be time
to do my hair
check my e-mail
write my opus
have a baby
acquire a career
erase my doubts

MORNING POEM #55

a walk through Chelsea
down an avenue
of ritzy restaurants
and high priced
clothing stores
perfecting the art
of tarrying
browse the used
bookstores
windowshop
notice the new
shops—be a tourist
in your own city
appreciate the big
lights—the strange signs
get fat, the Bowler
a taste of old New Orleans
the red red bar
Chinese and Cuban
restaurant row
who's dancing
at the Joyce
ogle *the food shop*
the new candle shop
down to the West Village
despairing over the
newly redecorated
Tiffany's, pausing

at *the Pleasure Chest*
then back Uptown
ignoring my favorite
Caffe Dell'Artista
for a home-cooked meal
and aching feet

MORNING POEM #56

fear of office work
creeping into my psyche
tomorrow: rush-hour crush
sitting behind someone else's
computer—biding time
or running back and
forth with busywork
paperwork, redtape
procedure, processing,
phone work, legwork
braindead work
5:00—time to go home

MORNING POEM #57

I am the catalyst
worlds whirl around me
fixed habits burn to cinders
new paths open and contract
and open again and again
lost children become stars
dead roads metamorphosize
I am the sand's irritant
working into pearl
an ankle bracelet
scratching skin as reminder
of connection, family
ties breaking walls
I am the directional
pull towards center
I am the savior of lost causes
the grace given the wayward
the open palm of plenitude
the Tao of the indecisive
I am the turner of pages
the alchemist of city grit
the waver of wands
the rocker of personal planets
I am the catalyst
for everyone
but myself

MORNING POEM #58

fluorescent honeycomb ceiling
rainbows the exit
space full of crisp right angles
brown, gray, blue
against white
off white
near white
green lights all in a row
three more hours til . . .
three more then end

MORNING POEM #59

forever in bed
waiting for heat
luring black cat
Tristana into trust

call for work
erasing dreams
wake up Joel and Tristana
and spritz a cloud
of Tatiana—rise and run
super stops on stairs
asking about the steam
about the heat
see former Mellow
Freakin' Woody on the way
handlebar moustache
a new addition
taking the shorter route
two stops and there
not more than two thoughts
in morning brain
forgot which company
forgot which boss
Fifth Ave. & Forty-Second
commuters frown
forgot to avoid
oncoming eyes
speed walk in a
comfortable daze
automatic movement
fine perception drowned
in self defense

noon already
morning gone
deadline extended
change plan
Friday: "Casual Day"
lists are in
feeling needed
by the folks
who jumble
the numbers
jumbling my
life/leisure
rearrange my art
to fit prosperity

MORNING POEM #62

at last I am myself
again—writing & reading
at 3 a.m. while others sleep
at home—at peace

MORNING POEM #63

completely out of time
he looked impossible
my nineteenth-century
gentleman with violet lids
& pale face closed in sleep

MORNING POEM #64

green screen
blue screen
erase the future
unseen
touch the invisible me
the double me
special FX
fantasy

MORNING POEM #65

sleep patterns
shifting—down late
up early
interrupted dreams

MORNING POEM #66

what's left to do
what's left
rain mists
in head
on pavement
check the lists
cross off
done done done
in back of mind
evening plans
guitar—singing
hot food/warm hearts

WANDA PHIPPS is a poet, performer, translator, and journalist. She received her B.A. in English with a Theater Concentration from Barnard College of Columbia University, studied poetry with Bernadette Mayer, Allen Ginsberg, and others at the Naropa Institute. Phipps also studied theater and acting at the American Conservatory Theatre in San Francisco. She is the author of the CD-ROM *Zither Mood* (Faux Press), the chapbooks *Lunch Poems* (Boog Literature), *Your Last Illusion or Break-Up Sonnets* (Situations Press), and *After the Mishap* (Faux Press). Her poems have appeared in more than sixty publications, including *Salon*, *Agni*, *Exquisite Corpse*, *How2*, *The World*, *Hanging Loose*, *Shampoo*, and *Boog Lit*. She has also been featured in the anthologies: *Verses That Hurt: Pleasure and Pain from the Poemfone Poets* (St. Martin's Press), *O•blek: Writing From the New Coast* (o•blek editions), *The Portable Boog Reader* (Boog Literature), and the *Boston Poetry Marathon 2003 Postcard Set* (Boog City). She is a contributing editor for *Big Bridge* and served on the editorial board of *Lungfull!* She has performed on stages all over the U.S. as a poet and with her various bands. Her poetry has been the subject of a short film entitled *Filmpoem for Wanda Phipps* by Joel Schlemowitz. *Wake-Up Calls: 66 Morning Poems* is her first full-length collection.